Hope in the Darkness

Hope in the Darkness

Finding the Light After the Trauma of Rape

Carrie Manke

Printed in the United States of America

ISBN: 978-1-946195-76-0
Library of Congress Control Number: 2020911302

Photo credit headshot: Richard Pederson, Richard Photographics, LLC

Cover Design & Interior Book Design: Ann Aubitz

Published by FuzionPress
1250 E 115th Street, Burnsville, MN 55337

To John, my guardian angel

INTRODUCTION

This is my story—the unfiltered and raw version of how my brain remembers my assault. I refer to it as *my* assault because it has become a part of me and has shaped the person I am today. My memory isn't completely accurate or logical at times, but this is how my brain sorted the information from that night and the years that followed. Most importantly, this book describes my journey—how I took one event that shaped my entire outlook on life and used it to help others.

As you read, I hope you'll realize that healing from horrific trauma, especially sexual trauma, *is possible*. Healing from something like this isn't easy, though. It's hard work, and there are setbacks, as you will see in my story.

Some names have been changed or omitted to protect those individuals' privacy.

Although many years have passed since my assault, I can still recall the night vividly.

It was a Friday night in June. I was heading out to meet a girlfriend I hadn't seen in a while. I remember that I didn't really want to go. We weren't very close, but I felt obligated to see her before heading out of town. My flight to California was less than two weeks away.

I was on summer break between my junior and senior years of college. I was planning to spend the summer in Hollywood and get my big break by going on countless auditions.

I had always dreamed of becoming an actress. Growing up, I acted in school plays, did community theater, and imagined my life as if it were a movie. Needless to say, I was a tad dramatic and was constantly "trying out for the part" as I went through my daily life. I knew that the only way I could really fulfill this dream was to move to Hollywood, because that was what all the big stars did.

My parents were reluctant for me to move to California for ten weeks, live in a hostel, and wander around Hollywood by myself. But they also wanted me to get this dream out of my system before I graduated with a "real" degree, so they couldn't argue with my plan.

Before heading out to the bar to meet my friend, I told my mom I wouldn't be out late. I was simply going to order a water, say hi, then leave.

I remember I was wearing jeans, flip-flops, a baseball cap, and my new and very stylish army fatigue jacket. I wasn't a girly girl, so it wasn't uncommon for me to dress like a tomboy.

I drove to the bar to meet my friend. I hadn't been to this area of Minneapolis before. Two paid parking lots were open, but I chose to park on the street, where it was free. I didn't see anyone around at the moment, but there were many parked cars, and I was only one block from the bar.

A semi was parked on the corner, and in front of it was an old boxy-looking red car. I pulled up in front of that car. The spot was somewhat dark. Several trees blocked the streetlights. I got out and walked around the front of my car, heading for the sidewalk. That was safer than walking on the fairly busy road.

I passed the red car and was nearing the front of the semi when I was suddenly attacked from behind. The man was shorter than me, so he had to jump on my back. He wrapped his arms around my neck, put a knife to my throat, and said, "Sh — don't scream, or I'll hurt you."

I believed him.

He dragged me to the red car and pushed me into the back seat. The thought going through my head was, *If I get into this car, I'm most likely never getting out.*

As he pushed me, I searched my purse blindly with one hand and found the police-grade mace on my keychain. He climbed in behind me, pushed me down, and sat on my legs. I couldn't move or get out the other door. However, I turned around and just started spraying. I managed to spray his face pretty well.

"What the fuck did you do to me?" he yelled as he closed the door behind him.

He quickly blindfolded me so I wouldn't see his face, though I caught a glimpse. He looked Latino. Then he somehow took off my clothes. He sat on my legs the entire time so I couldn't get up.

My memory gets disjointed at this point. I remember talking to him the entire time I was in the car. I knew he was going to rape me, so I tried to convince him not to. I told him I had STDs, HIV. I told him I would do other things rather than be raped. I remember I was on my period, so he had to pull out my tampon.

At some point, my phone rang. I had just downloaded the *Inspector Gadget* theme song as my ringtone. It had been one of my favorite shows growing up, and I had been ecstatic to find the ringtone. He grabbed my phone from my purse, read my friend's name on the caller ID out loud, laughed, and threw it on the floor.

I heard voices outside at one point. People were walking by the car, but I couldn't tell how close they were. From what I could hear, they were no farther than the other side of the street.

He put the knife to my neck again, covered my mouth with his other hand, and reminded me not to scream or he would hurt me. I contemplated trying to scream or get out of the car, but I believed him again.

Somewhere in the process of being in the car and getting raped, I was stabbed in the neck and abdomen and nicked in a few other places, including my eyebrow. I didn't feel anything.

My body had no sensation, but I could hear. He had broken English and spoke in sentences with only a few words. I listened carefully to his voice and continued to plead with him not to rape me.

After he was done with me, he repeated, "What the fuck did you do to me? You stupid bitch."

His face was burning from the mace. I had gotten a little bit of mace on my hand from spraying him. It hurt like hell, so I can't imagine what his face felt like.

He wouldn't let me go because he thought I would go to the police. "You saw me," he said. "You saw my face. You tell police."

I tried to convince him I wouldn't tell and that I didn't see his face, even though I had seen it briefly before he got the blindfold on. He was angry and kept moaning about his face burning. I repeated that I wouldn't tell the police. I begged for him to let me go.

He then tied my hands together with something. It was so tight that it cut off my circulation. He tightened the blindfold. I heard him climb over the front seat, and then the car started moving.

This was my chance to escape. I was going to wait until he stopped, count to five, somehow get out the door with my hands tied together, and just start running.

I also thought about trying to roll out of the car while it was moving. But I was completely naked and had no idea where we were. I had parked on a side street, but there was a fair amount of traffic in the area on a Friday night. I was afraid I would get run over if I rolled out of the car. Then again, I remember thinking that getting seriously injured might be a better option than what he had planned for me.

As I went back and forth on what my best option was, he stopped the car a few times. Through the blindfold, I saw the dome light turn on. I heard him open the front door, then quickly close it and keep on driving. I later found out he was disposing of my clothes and purse along the road.

The car took an abrupt turn and stopped. I heard him get out. I remember seeing light through the blindfold — streetlights, perhaps. I prayed we were in a public place. I started counting to five.

He opened the back door and dragged me out. He shoved me. "Walk. Don't look. Keep walking."

I felt pavement and gravel underneath my feet. I started walking slowly. I was still blindfolded, and I had no idea where I was. I didn't know what I could be walking into or if I would end up falling off a bridge.

I heard the car door slam and the screeching of tires. I continued to walk for what I think was ten seconds. Then I turned around. I managed to pull off my blindfold and saw my hands were tied together with my bra.

I saw no one. I was in a deserted parking lot.

I started running out of the parking lot, toward the street. Suddenly, I looked down and realized my pants were around one ankle. I hadn't even felt them until that moment. I stopped to pull up my pants, then I kept running. I untied my hands as I ran.

I looked down and saw blood all over my abdomen. I started to regain some sensation. I realized the left side of my neck had a little discomfort, so I put my hand up to it. It felt sticky. I looked at my hand and saw a ton of blood.

I kept running. I started down the street, not knowing where I was or how far he had driven me.

I grew up Christian and was pretty active in youth group. In college, I continued practicing my faith by attending a Bible study and a Fellowship of Christian Athletes weekly service. I believed that Jesus died for my sins and that I was going to heaven.

However, I didn't believe miracles actually happened, aside from the time Jesus was on earth. And I was even skeptical about those miracles. I definitely didn't believe God sent angels to help us.

My beliefs were flipped upside down that night.

I met an angel.

As I was running down the street, I saw a big garage door open to a manufacturing warehouse. There was light coming from inside, which I found strange for a Friday night. Thinking there may be people inside, I hurried toward it. I couldn't run fast because the gravel on the road was thick and unstable.

As I came up the road, a man suddenly appeared from the shadows. He had been sitting on the curb outside the garage door, smoking a cigarette. I stopped immediately and backed away, thinking he was going to hurt me.

The look on his face changed from confusion to horror as he saw I was half-naked and bloody all over my abdomen and hands. He stopped, immediately took off his shirt, and reached out to hand it to me. I don't remember if he said anything, but I know he didn't come close to me. I imagine I looked terrified.

Suddenly, other men were around. One was on the phone. Within minutes, I heard a siren down the street. The fire truck came first, and soon after, a police car came speeding down the street. Then the ambulance arrived. Firemen, policemen, and male paramedics swarmed me and started asking me questions.

I don't remember if I said anything. But I know I didn't let them touch me.

This is where my memory gets really fuzzy. My memory comes in bursts, similar to how you see a person coming in and out of consciousness on a TV show. As they open their eyes, you see a flash of white light or a blurry image on the screen. For a bit, the show continues as if the camera is their eyes. But then there's another flash of white light or blurriness, and they slip back into unconsciousness.

I don't remember getting in the ambulance, riding to the hospital, or where I ended up. I remember lying on my back and looking up at bright lights. I was surrounded by people. Someone started cutting off my pants. I was very aware that I was exposed, and that meant danger.

I remember a woman with long brown hair standing on my right side. She had a concerned and caring look on her face. On my other side was a male officer who kept asking me questions.

"Where's my mom?" I asked the kind woman.

She told me my mom was on the way.

I started to cry. But then I immediately stopped myself. I still wasn't safe. I needed to stay alert and strong. My mom was safety. And until she got there, I wasn't safe.

I was rolled on the cart out of the trauma bay. I saw my mom and dad standing outside the doors to the stabilization room.

I asked the nurse to tell my parents what had happened. I couldn't tell my mom myself—I knew it would break her. She had been sexually assaulted by her brother as a kid. She had made it her life mission to never let that happen to her girls. I felt like I had failed her.

My mom is a very stoic person. The look on her face was something I had never seen before. Later, she told me that she literally collapsed. My dad had to catch her.

I had a sexual assault exam later that night. I don't remember much of it. I remember the sexual assault nurse's face. She had a soft, kind expression and short blond hair. She was holding a Polaroid camera.

I remember I was naked, sitting on a table, and she was taking pictures of me. She took a lot of photos of my chest, because he had bitten my breast.

Incidentally, I don't remember the pelvic exam at all.

My next memory is of my hand burning from the mace while I was upstairs in the hospital room for the night. I wanted to keep it in the ice water they had given me, but they told me I couldn't. The second I took it out of the ice water, it felt as if it were on fire.

My mom and sisters were there. I remember my sister washed between my legs because I had blood all over from my period. I don't remember sleeping, but I remember that my mom stayed with me overnight.

In the morning, they had to do some sort of x-ray to determine if the stab wound to my neck had caused any internal damage to my blood vessels. The only part of the test I remember is that the two female technicians had trouble getting my earrings out and that the board I had to lean against was freezing cold.

I do recall seeing my boyfriend, Jay, before leaving the hospital. My parents had called him, and he flew overnight from out of state to come see me. He lived in Colorado but was in California to have jaw surgery. He had just arrived in California when he got the call from my parents. His surgery was scheduled for Monday, so he came for forty-eight hours to spend time with me.

I took my first shower that Saturday afternoon at my parents' house. I felt so vulnerable—I couldn't handle being naked. I had to ask Jay to sit in the bathroom with me while I showered.

My parents let Jay and me sleep in my sister's bedroom, because she had a queen-size bed and I only had a twin. I don't remember crying or talking much, but I do remember lying on my side in bed, staring at Jay. I was numb—emotionally and physically. I don't know what my face looked like. When I bring myself back to that weekend, I remember staring with a blank expression and emptiness behind my eyes. I was in complete shock, as if I had seen a ghost.

That Monday, I had to go to the police station. My mom drove me, but they wouldn't let her stay with me.

I was escorted into a small room, approximately ten feet by five feet. A table took up most of the space. A man with a mustache sat across from me at the table, and there was a video camera behind him. He told me everything I said would be recorded, then he asked me to tell him what happened.

I don't remember what I said, but I do remember thinking, *Why do I have to tell you?* and *When can I get out of this room?*

The man with the mustache wasn't threatening, but I didn't trust him or the situation. I was in an enclosed space with a man who could hurt me. I recall seeing two doors, but I could be imagining that because I felt so threatened. I've learned that some of my memories aren't very accurate.

I wanted to draw a picture of the man who assaulted me. The man with the mustache took some descriptors from me but wouldn't bring in a sketch artist. My mom told me a few years later that they didn't trust my memory of the man who raped me because I was blindfolded for most of it.

I felt I had enough memory of his face to draw a sketch, but the police didn't agree. The most prominent things I remember were that his face was round, his skin color was yellowish, and his ears were very distinct. They were kind of folded in.

After I finished telling the man with the mustache what I remembered, he brought me into another room. In my memory, I picture it as kind of circular with several doors around it.

Again, I don't know if my memory is accurate, but I do know that I was and still am keenly aware of where doors are located. I know the fastest exit from any room, including restaurants, movie theaters, and classrooms. I rarely sit with my back to an exit, and I get anxious sitting in the middle of a row in church or in a theater. I need to have a quick path to get out.

It's not claustrophobia. I can handle lying in the narrow tube for an MRI test, and I can stay calm in crowded elevators, as long as I'm not near the back. But seat me at a restaurant table with my back to a hallway or bathroom entrance, and my fight-or-flight response will kick in. I need to be able to see what's happening behind me.

A female officer met me in the circular room. She directed me to a smaller room and said she was going to take photos of my injuries. My most prominent injuries were my neck wound, which was now covered in stitches; my abdomen wound, which was covered in a bandage; and the bruising on my breasts, which was still freshly blue and purple.

The officer made me lift my shirt so she could take photos of my breast and stomach. The door to the room was still open, and she was standing in the doorway. There was no one else in the circular room, but I was confused about why she didn't close the door for privacy. Even with the door closed, I would have felt somewhat safe with a woman in that enclosed space. I knew that if I had to escape, I could push her over and run out of the circular room.

I remember only snippets from that summer. I was in complete shock as I entered the first stage of post-traumatic stress disorder (PTSD). Getting raped wasn't the biggest issue—it was the realization that I could have died.

When people have near-death experiences, it changes their brains and how they look at the world. Many people go through PTSD after near-death experiences. This includes everyone from people who have been assaulted to people who almost died from cardiac arrest. Even those who experience vicarious trauma—paramedics, police officers, and nurses—experience some form of PTSD.

After a near-death experience, your whole outlook changes as you attempt to figure out what's really important in life and how to live with purpose. Though I struggled for a few years, this eventually became my mindset. It still is at the forefront of my mind. I vow to live each day as if it's my last — because it very well could be. I check items off my bucket list on a regular basis. I don't let experiences pass me by.

I obviously didn't go to California that summer. I don't recall even leaving the house much. I worked at a pool store, testing water and selling chemicals. I needed to work. It was my only sense of normalcy, and it helped me integrate back into my life.

The only memory I have from work that summer is freaking out at a coworker for touching me. She was just being playful, but I went ballistic on her. Thankfully, everyone at work cut me some slack. They could have called me crazy and told me not to come back to work.

A difficult aspect of the healing process was learning to determine which places were safe. The night of my rape, I had thought the area I parked in was safe. I'd had no concerns walking down the street at 8:00 p.m. because it was a populated area that didn't have a high crime rate. But then my sense of safety was shattered.

I struggled with this for a couple of years. My mom has told me that I once drove to the mall but couldn't get out of the car, so I drove back home. I didn't know if walking from my car to the mall in broad daylight was safe.

That summer, I went to visit Jay in Colorado for a week. He was recovering from his jaw surgery. Being able to eat only liquids was challenging for him. He was already a skinny guy, so he had to make sure to get in enough calories.

We went to P.F. Chang's a few times to get containers of hot-and-sour soup. I also made him creative meals in a blender, including ground-up chicken and soups. I put three to four scoops of protein powder in everything I made.

With the first blended meal, he kept telling me it tasted like protein powder. I lied and said I put in only one scoop.

"You must be sensitive to the taste of it," I told him.

After the second blended meal, he started saying, "This is really good."

I secretly laughed, knowing that half the glass was full of protein powder!

We didn't do much during that week, but it was perfect. Jay was so kind to me and did anything I needed.

I felt guilty for sleeping twelve to thirteen hours a night. I had flown out to see him, yet I spent half the day in bed.

My brain was trying to sort through memories and heal, so sleeping that much was necessary. My sleep was not restful, though; I had nightmares every night.

I was also sleepy because I had started taking a new medication for my migraines. I had experienced occasional migraines prior to my assault, but they were constant after. I went to three neurologists, and one told me, "It's all in your head. You just need to get over it and move on." I tried many medications that summer.

After my assault, I underwent intensive therapy at the prodding of my parents. My mom drove me every week. I was scared to walk from the car into the building and up the stairs to the therapist's office. The office was located in a part of Minneapolis I had never been to before. I didn't know if it was safe.

I also didn't want to go because the therapist made me talk about that horrific night. She was trained to work with trauma survivors. Eventually, I started getting some benefit from it.

The therapy I found most helpful was Eye Movement Desensitization and Reprocessing (EMDR). It's unclear to psychologists how it works, exactly, but it essentially creates new pathways in the brain when you recall a traumatic event.

Triggers can be visual, olfactory, auditory, or even emotional. They make the brain quickly access traumatic memories along electrical pathways. The second your brain senses a trigger, it remembers there is something associated with it. For example, if you smell pies in the oven, it instantly reminds you of Thanksgiving. This usually occurs in the nonlogical part of your brain. This is the basis of flashbacks.

My biggest trigger is personal space. I am keenly aware of people behind me. The hair on my neck stands up when someone comes within three feet of my back, even if I don't hear or see them.

This reaction can happen anywhere. If someone is standing too close to my back when I'm in line at a store, I immediately react—my brain remembers my assault and thinks I'm in danger. I go into fight-or-flight mode. I've had to leave places because I freak out and can't breathe when my sympathetic nervous system gets activated.

EMDR works to access those traumatic events and essentially rewire the pathway. The trained therapist works your brain to send signals across the hemispheres. So, if your traumatic memory isn't stored in the logical part of your brain, the rewiring works to input logic into the memory.

After rewiring these pathways and teaching my brain that, say, standing in line at a store isn't a dangerous situation, I can better control this trigger. I've learned how to adjust to the situation with logic rather than with fight-or-flight.

So, you will often see me standing sideways in a line when people are too close. Or I take a step to the side. I do whatever I have to do to not have someone too close to my back. In my head, I'm saying, "I'm safe. I'm safe. I'm safe."

One of the best tools I learned in therapy is that I am in control of my flashbacks. I describe flashbacks like a video: Your brain senses a trigger, then pushes Play, and you are forced to watch a portion of the traumatic event. You have no control over when this happens or how long the video will play. You become paralyzed. You have no awareness of your body or your emotions. It's almost as if the world around you has frozen in time.

Through therapy, I've learned that I have two options when a trigger causes my brain to push Play: One, I can watch the video at that moment, if I so choose. Or two, I can choose to watch it a little later, when I feel more comfortable, safe, and prepared.

There is no third option, though, to not watch it at all. I can push the video out for a few hours. But if I don't eventually allow my brain to watch it, the triggers will keep coming and my brain will keep pushing Play.

This technique has helped me get through work and social situations. It takes practice, but it allows me to feel like I have more control over the experience.

Ten years after my assault, I was asked to share my story at a local conference. I sat down to put my memories into words on a page, so I allowed my brain to push Play. Tears were streaming down my face the entire time I was typing. I couldn't control the emotions that came along with watching the video in my mind.

Every time I recall my rape, there is a component of sadness and grief. But I am also thankful to be alive and to have the strength to help others as a result of my experience. The more I have talked about my rape and presented my story, the less intense my emotions are when I play the video.

Many survivors struggle with flashbacks and symptoms of PTSD because they aren't able to get control. I don't blame them. Flashbacks are the natural way your brain tries to protect you. If we encounter a life-or-death situation, our brain is designed to remember it so we can avoid it in the future. It uses triggers and flashbacks to help us learn from our experiences.

For example, if a lion tried to attack you, your brain would remember, "I need to run," every time you saw a lion. This trigger would fire, and your body would take action before you consciously realized why you were running.

I realize that I will probably never have a "normal" or "healthy" brain. I will always have triggers because my brain will always try to protect me. But I am thankful that therapy allowed me to recognize these triggers and bring in logic.

Again, one of my triggers is someone standing too close behind me in line. I can now recognize my physical reactions to that trigger. My heart rate rises, I get stiff as my muscles warm up, and my senses heighten.

But because I have rewired these pathways in my brain, I can now bring logic into the situation. My logical brain tells my body, "You can relax. This isn't a threatening situation." I can then take a deep breath and slow my sympathetic nervous system. Instead of fight-or-flight, I can take action by turning sideways, so the person is no longer directly behind me. I can also continue to tell myself "I'm safe" until my heart rate returns to normal.

The most challenging emotion I had to work through in therapy was blame. I blamed myself for not screaming, for not trying to run before getting in the car, and for not trying to get out of the car before getting raped and stabbed.

This is a perfect example of how my memory does not include logic. Any person who hears my story says, "Of course you didn't do those things. You thought you were going to die—and you could have, if you had done those things."

My brain did not see it that way in the beginning. But through EMDR, I've realized that I did what I needed to do at the time in order to get out alive. I could go through what-ifs all day long, but it will do me no good.

In that life-threatening moment, I obviously believed he was capable of hurting me—and he did. I had no control over how I reacted. I still have no idea how I even thought to use the mace as my one chance to escape. I also don't know how I remained calm after the mace didn't stop him. The police have told me that's probably why I survived. Had I thrashed around or fought back more, he probably would have killed me.

I started back up at St. Olaf for my senior year in September. I could hardly function. Campus security had to drive me to all my classes because I couldn't handle walking outside, even during the day. I couldn't be in rooms without multiple exits, or I had to at least sit or stand near an exit.

I was entering the second and third phases of PTSD: feeling numb and depressed and having flashbacks. I had flashbacks constantly and horrible nightmares. I could barely keep up with classes or homework. I had to drop a class that semester.

Every week, I also had to drive back home for physical therapy for my neck. I was extremely lucky to not have serious injuries from my stab wound, but my neck had gotten really tight from favoring the right side over the left. I didn't want to move it, because it hurt.

At the prompt of my therapist, I joined a PTSD support group for rape survivors. But because stranger rapes make up a small percentage of sexual assaults, I felt isolated and angry that no one understood what I went through. All the women in the group had experienced intimate-partner sexual abuse, incest, or date rape. I also felt isolated because I was the youngest there. Most of them were in their thirties or forties.

I internally rolled my eyes when they talked about how scared they were of their boyfriends or husbands and that they didn't feel like they could run away. I wanted to yell, "But did he have a knife to your throat? All you have to do is punch him and run out the door! You continue to go back home every day and subject yourself to this abuse. What's wrong with you? You are choosing to be assaulted. *I* didn't have a choice."

I told my therapist that this support group was not going to help me. None of their experiences came close to mine. None of them had almost died.

But my therapist was firm. He told me I had to keep going in order to heal.

I soon learned that even though those women and I had different rape stories, we all experienced the same emotions. PTSD and the process of recovery is universal for traumatic events.

I spent the first couple of years after my assault with victim mentality, as I'd call it, and a lot of anger. I hated God for letting this happen to me. I was angry with the world for the evil that exists and for the fact that no one does anything to stop it.

I was angry with the police because they screwed up trying to find the man who raped me. I wasn't the only one angry. The sergeant in sex crimes at the Minneapolis Police Department was furious when he found out how the police handled the situation that night.

The man who raped me used my cell phone for a couple of days. He sent pictures of his genitalia to my recent contacts, including my mom, my boyfriend, and the friend I was going to meet that night. Although they didn't have the "find my phone" technology we have today, they still could have traced my phone to a small radius.

In one of the photos he sent, a poster was hanging in the background. It was a unique poster from Mexico, one that isn't widely available. The police didn't care to investigate that lead either.

The sexual assault nurse examiner got DNA evidence from me, and it matched another assault in the national DNA database. It was a similar situation: a woman had been raped at knifepoint by a stranger in her car one morning. She had not been stabbed, though. The fact that he stabbed me meant he was escalating.

The neighborhood where the other woman had been raped was close to Minneapolis. With that location and the location of my rape, the police had an idea of where he possibly lived. But even though I gave them a pretty good description of his car, they never searched that neighborhood for it.

He still has not been caught. My rape is considered a cold case, and they run the DNA through the database every six months. The police believe he is either dead or has moved back to Mexico (if that is where he was from) because there haven't been any more DNA hits.

However, that doesn't necessarily mean he has stopped raping women. Not everyone reports.

I sometimes fantasize about what I would do to him if he were caught. It's quite graphic, so I'll spare you the details. There's a line of people behind me who want a piece of him.

But I get him first.

I'm not sure how I got through my senior year at St. Olaf. I wasn't sure what I wanted to do with myself after graduation.

Unfortunately, things didn't work out with Jay. He was one year younger than me, so he planned to be in Minnesota for another year but then move back home to Colorado for grad school. He wanted to become a lawyer.

I was contemplating a master's in social work, but I knew that I didn't want to move to Colorado. I wanted to stay close to home. I was lost and couldn't figure out my purpose in life. While I was finishing my last semester of college, Jay was studying abroad. I feel like we drifted apart that spring.

In retrospect, he was an amazing boyfriend and would have made a wonderful husband. But it wasn't in God's plan, or it would have worked out.

I will be forever indebted to him for everything he did to help me heal. Because of Jay, I don't have problems with intimacy or sex. He was gentle and understanding. He never pushed me to do anything physical that made me uncomfortable. Jay is the reason I was able to get married.

As my senior year came to a close that spring, I managed to go on job interviews and land a job, which I started one week after graduation. I credit my therapist and family for helping me get through that year and continue on with my life goals.

I got a job in sales, something in which I always had an interest. I enjoyed sales and was a natural at it. I sold the most candy bars for high school fundraising events, and I even made some commissions on products I sold at my summer job at the pool store. I also had an interest in pharmaceuticals and the medical field, so I imagined I would work at this entry-level sales job for a while before landing my dream job as a pharmaceutical sales rep.

After a few months, however, I found the job unfulfilling and hated going to work. I couldn't imagine finding joy in selling anything at this point—pharmaceuticals included.

The medical field still fascinated me, but I didn't know what I wanted to do. I had taken many premed classes in college because I liked science. I thought about becoming a doctor, but that didn't feel like the right fit. I shadowed a surgeon and went on an ambulance ride-along, but these also didn't feel like good fits.

My dad, rightfully so, was frustrated that he had spent thousands of dollars on an education gone to waste. I had a math degree but didn't want to do sales, teach, be an actuary or accountant, or do any other "boring" job.

He set me up with a career counselor, and I took several aptitude and personality tests. Not surprisingly, the results showed I had an interest in health-care roles. I scored a high interest in optometry and nursing.

I don't get excited about eyeballs, so the counselor suggested I consider becoming a nurse.

I told her, quite frankly, "Hell no. I don't want to be a doctor's bitch."

She looked perplexed and asked me what I thought nurses did.

"They take orders from doctors and get them coffee," I replied.

"That might be what they did in the 1940s," she explained. "But nurses do a lot more these days." She encouraged me to speak with nurses to learn more about the profession.

I interviewed a couple of nurses in different areas of health care to figure out what they really did every day. After learning more, I decided to give it a chance.

I didn't realize it at the time, but nursing was my calling.

So, I left my stable job with a reasonable salary and took a job earning slightly more than minimum wage as a nursing assistant. I enrolled in nursing school prerequisite classes and fell in love with the profession. I loved going to class and learning about the body. My grades were even better than when I was an undergraduate.

I was excited to start my career as a nurse and help people. I eagerly applied to nursing schools—only to get turned down seven times.

I revisited the anger emotion and blamed the world. Why did I have to encounter so many obstacles, after what I had already gone through? If nursing was God's plan for me, why was it so difficult to get into nursing school?

At the time, there weren't many bachelor's-to-bachelor's programs in Minnesota. They all had different requirements and start dates. You need a BSN as a baseline for higher degrees in nursing, which I knew I would want to pursue at some point. I decided I didn't want to get an associate's degree and then have to spend more time getting my BSN. I wanted to go straight to a BSN program.

I was frustrated that I couldn't get into any Minnesota schools, so I started looking out of state. Part of me also wanted to move out of state because I never got to experience that summer in California.

I applied to NYU on a whim; I thought it would be fun to live in New York City. I was accepted, but then I learned it would cost me $150,000 for the program plus living expenses for fifteen months. It would have been a fun, challenging experience to live in New York, but it wasn't realistic to spend that much money on a bachelor's degree. I cried when I sent my declination in the mail.

After looking at a minimum of fifty schools throughout the US, I made a decision matrix. That's how I make all decisions—with logic! I ranked schools based on cost, number of prerequisite classes I would have to take, location, cost of living, length of the program, and reputation.

There was a twelve-month accelerated BSN program at Saint Louis University in Missouri. It was the shortest program, the cost of living was low, I had taken all the prerequisite courses, and it was affordable. St. Louis wasn't high on my travel list, but it was a big city with lots to offer, and the weather was warmer than Minnesota's.

I applied and got in instantly. Moving out of state was a test for me. I was scared to not have my safety net, but I knew I needed to push myself to continue to heal.

One of the most difficult things about moving was the challenge it posed to my sense of safety. I had rebuilt my sense of safety over the past four years in Minneapolis, so I felt somewhat confident in my judgment. However, most of St. Louis was unsafe, with a high crime rate. I had to be careful. (As it turned out, someone was robbed at gunpoint outside my apartment building.) Still, I knew moving was a good way to push myself to heal even more.

It helped, too, that I had this feeling that I was invincible. *I've had my one and done – what else can happen to me?* I thought. I still kind of feel this way, though I certainly don't put myself in dangerous situations.

When I got to nursing school, I soon realized this *was* my calling. I had never been so passionate about anything in my life. I learned more about forensic nursing and made a promise to myself that I would someday work with sexual assault survivors.

Nursing school actually helped me heal from my assault. Learning about how the brain works when it encounters trauma helped me understand why I went through PTSD and why I get flashbacks.

I also learned about abuse and how to recognize the signs in others—even though I ironically couldn't recognize the signs in my own life. At twenty-six, I married a classic abuser. Charming and apologetic.

I divorced him when I was thirty, but even then, it took me three years after that to realize I had been abused.

Then memories came flooding back, and I was able to connect the dots.

I had ignored many red flags while dating him. For example, he twisted my arm one day because he wasn't happy with something I had said. He once slammed my fingers in a door—I don't even remember why.

When I graduated from nursing school, I got a job in a long-term care facility back in Minneapolis. I got married that fall. The following July, my then husband made us move to Philadelphia, isolating me from my family and friends.

I still wonder why I married him. I attribute some of it to my assault. I met him two years after my assault; my brain wasn't completely healed. My brain didn't know how to decipher between healthy love and unhealthy love.

In Philadelphia, I started working in an emergency department (ED). The ED became my home. My brain is wired to handle trauma, so I thrive in an urban ED.

I also took the class to become a sexual assault nurse. I was finally in a mental state where I could work with survivors. I loved it.

Even though I can't save people from trauma like what I went through, I can be there for them emotionally and mentally when they come into the ED. I know what it's like to be in the ED on the worst day of your life. I can relate to patients on a different level, especially those with near-death traumatic experiences.

It has become my life mission to help others and save lives. I used to dream about seeing women being raped and saving them. I've beat up a lot of men in dreams. I know that God kept me alive to save lives and share my story.

About a year after our move, my then husband's job switched back to Minnesota. Through phone interviews from Philadelphia, I landed a job in the ED at Hennepin County Medical Center (HCMC) in Minneapolis.

My therapist in Philadelphia told me I was crazy for choosing that hospital—it was where I had been brought that night. I couldn't recall much of my stay at HCMC, so she was worried that memories would start coming back and that I would have flashbacks.

I told her I wanted to work at a Level I trauma center in the Twin Cities and I wouldn't let my experience stop me from following my dreams. But obviously, I did have some anxiety, and I worked through more EMDR therapy prior to moving back.

Because of the timing of the move, my first day at HCMC was my first official day on the job. I didn't have time to tour the hospital prior to starting. And what my therapist predicted came true. I had flashbacks daily for at least three months, and I felt as if I were in a trance every day.

The first time I walked into the stabilization room, I had an immense flashback and had to walk out. Time was frozen, and the video of that night was playing. Some memories started coming back about when I had been brought to the stabilization room.

Because of therapy, I knew how to handle flashbacks. I felt more in control over them. So to work through my flashbacks, I purposely made myself walk into the stabilization room periodically when it was empty. I often told my brain it was not the right time to watch the video or think about this. After work, though, I spent a lot of time reflecting and allowing myself to feel the reoccurring emotions.

Over time, it got easier. I eventually had no issues working in there.

When I started at HCMC, I didn't tell anyone what had happened to me. I didn't want people to worry that my assault affected my work performance.

However, when I later opened up to my coworkers, they admitted that it did actually affect my performance. It didn't affect how I performed my actual duties as a nurse, but it did affect how I carried out my interpersonal skills. As they explained it, I was not the friendliest person. They told me I didn't say hello to people and didn't make eye contact when passing someone in the hallway. It's because I was in a complete trance as my brain was constantly trying to press Play to remember my rape.

After some memories started coming back, I became obsessed with figuring out what else had happened to me in the hospital that night. I requested my chart from the medical records department so I could try to piece together my disjointed memories.

I went down in my scrubs with my employee badge on. I asked the medical records staff member to send me a copy of my chart from my visit on June 3, 2005. This was the only time I had been seen at HCMC.

She looked at the computer screen and obviously saw the chief complaint for my visit to the ED. She looked back at me with wide eyes.

"You want the entire chart?"

"Yes," I said with a smile.

My chart didn't include the sexual assault exam. I haven't pursued obtaining it. I may at some point, but part of me doesn't want to read it. Knowing the details of my exam and what I said during it might be more traumatic than it's worth.

The chart didn't help me piece together memories, but it was fascinating to view my hospital stay from a medical perspective. My sympathetic nervous system was activated, as my vital signs reflected. My blood pressure, pulse, and blood sugar were high. I was given pain medication, even though I don't remember being in pain. It's also noted in my chart that I didn't say much to the staff and was "withdrawn."

Reading my chart was educational. I could see the direct effects trauma has on the body. Understanding trauma helps one understand why survivors can't give logical, succinct statements that follow a timeline.

The memory of my assault still isn't logical. Over the years, I've asked my mom to read my notes for the presentation I give about trauma and my assault. The first time she read them, she told me that parts of my recollection are incorrect and out of order. Some of my memories don't make a ton of sense or miss context, but I can't make my brain remember them any differently.

I also learned new information from my mom's feedback. For instance, I learned that my family members all went through counseling that summer and that my dad was the one who stayed with me in the hospital overnight.

The only time I remember seeing my dad at the hospital was right before my sexual assault exam, when I came out of the stabilization room. I can't figure out why I would block the memory of my dad being there, but the brain does amazing things to cope.

I soon started working as a sexual assault nurse for HCMC. The program there is excellent, and I'm very thankful to have been a part of it. I learned a lot more about sexual assaults, trauma, and how to become a better forensic nurse. I'm fascinated by how trauma affects the brain.

People who know my story ask me all the time, "Isn't that hard for you? Don't you have flashbacks?"

It's actually therapeutic for me to work with survivors. Even though most sexual assaults I've seen aren't stranger rapes, all survivors go through similar emotions. I can *feel* what they're feeling. Without saying much, I can be physically, emotionally, and mentally there for them. Some survivors have actually asked me during exams if I've been raped. I think they can sense it.

I've completed only one exam where I had a flashback experience. She had been hit on the head with a crowbar from behind and stranger-raped. She was in complete shock when she came to me. I imagine that's what I looked like during my exam.

After doing that exam, I spent time reflecting on my assault and talked about it with my family. Even though I don't think about it every day and I've worked through all the stages of PTSD, I still need to talk about it sometimes.

I've also developed a sixth sense when it comes to abuse. On multiple occasions, I have encountered someone I knew was being abused, even if they didn't tell me. I have told ED providers, "I know the patient denied it or hasn't admitted it, but they're being abused at home." The providers look at me like I'm crazy.

I can't save everyone. But maybe I can be that one person who gives a patient the opportunity to talk about their experience with abuse.

I started looking at grad school options in 2013. From the beginning, I knew I would pursue a graduate degree in nursing. I'm an overachiever, and I love school!

I've always been curious about how things work, and I've always asked a lot of thought-provoking questions. I was the kid who asked her parents, "Why is the sky blue?" After years of annoying questions, they finally bought me a *101 Questions and Answers to Everything You Want to Know* book. It was perfect!

I also like making things more efficient. Inefficiency drives me crazy. I constantly strive to make myself and everything around me better. I want my patients to have good outcomes.

Nurses are creative and innovative. They sometimes have to cut corners, because there's never enough time to get everything done. So when I worked as a bedside nurse in the ED, I frequently thought about ways we could do things differently to make it more efficient for nurses and safer for patients.

I thought a career as an acute care nurse practitioner would be a good fit. I could work with trauma patients and essentially practice like a doctor, which had been one of my potential career paths.

When I looked into the Doctor of Nursing Practice program at the University of Minnesota, I learned there were more than nurse practitioner options. I clicked on the link for clinical nurse specialist (CNS) and started reading about that program. The description was kind of vague, so I also googled it.

A website popped up that included the words "safety, quality improvement, and efficiency." I stared at the computer screen and thought, *There's a degree in nursing out there for my personality!*

I shadowed a CNS and learned they have a broad scope of practice. I discovered that I could practice like an acute care nurse practitioner as well as work on quality improvement initiatives to increase patient safety and improve patient outcomes.

I entered the CNS program at the University of Minnesota. I got my highest GPA in my doctoral program. My GPA increased with every degree, interestingly. When I find passion in something, I excel in it.

My first job was working as a medical-surgical CNS in a Level I trauma center. I questioned why they wanted me to take the job because I had never worked on a medical-surgical unit in a hospital.

I ended up enjoying my job, and I learned a lot about the inpatient world of nursing. CNSs have the unique ability to research and appraise evidence, so if I didn't know an answer, I could look it up. My skill set focuses on improving patient outcomes by implementing best practices based on evidence, so the population I work with doesn't matter.

Still, I'm an ED nurse through and through. I want to be there for patients on the worst days of their lives.

So when I was asked to be the ED CNS at a different Level I trauma center in the Twin Cities, I jumped at the opportunity. I didn't even know a job like that could exist. I could work as a bedside RN, gain insight about nursing practice in the ED, and then impact patient outcomes on a large scale.

I missed working with sexual assault survivors, but I still encountered enough trauma patients to fill that bucket. Just being back in the ED reignited my passion for nursing and why I'm on earth.

T hen again, perhaps nursing isn't my forever role. Sometimes I feel called to be a missionary.

I went on a mission trip to Haiti in 2014 and have been going almost every year since then. These missions provide both medical support and Christian-based life transformation to underserved communities.

One can read about health disparities in the news, but to interact with the people who live through these disparities is a whole different experience. I held a twenty-eight-day-old baby who would die in a few days because his parents couldn't get him to the hospital. I cared for young children with foodborne illnesses from not having clean water.

Women came to the clinic with complaints of nausea and fatigue. They had no way of knowing they were pregnant and didn't understand that sex led to pregnancy.

Young women and men sought care for STDs because they didn't have access to condoms.

Daily trauma from physical and sexual abuse is the norm for many people in Haiti. People are expected to turn the other way when they see or hear it happening next door.

I have so much to offer the underserved populations of the world. God saved my life so that I could help others.

Ironically, I became atheist for a while after my assault. I was so angry and didn't believe God would let something like this happen to me. Why didn't he intervene? Why didn't he tell one of the people walking by the car to look in and save me? Why did he even let me go out that night?

I will never know the answers to these questions. But I do know that God doesn't *want* bad things to happen to us.

A pastor helped me rekindle my faith. "God didn't abandon you that night," she said. "He was there with you, crying, holding you."

I've stopped asking why and started focusing on the impact God has made on me as a result of this experience.

I wouldn't have been able to get through nursing school without support from God. I wouldn't be able to speak publicly about my experience without strength from God. I wouldn't have been able to write this book without God.

Amazingly, I have learned to forgive the man who raped me. Fred Luskin's forgiveness theory has been very helpful. Anger, hurt, and resentment harm only yourself. They build up stress in your body and then impact your physical health.

Forgiveness isn't for the other person. Learning to forgive is a weight off your own shoulders because you don't have to carry those detrimental, unhealthy emotions anymore. It's also important to note that forgiveness doesn't mean that what the other person did was OK.

I've shared my story at several sexual assault nurse trainings. One time, the program coordinator requested that my mom speak with me. My mom was nervous but felt her version of the story was important for people to hear. She talked about her healing that summer and how my assault brought up childhood emotions from her experience with rape.

During the question-and-answer portion of our presentation, a woman asked if I'd ever reconnected with my angel, the man who had helped me that night.

"I don't have his contact information," I answered.

My mom then stated, "I do."

My eyes got wide and I froze.

"I've told you this several times, but you never seem to remember it," my mom said.

As my mom had already explained in the presentation, I've asked her the same questions over the years, but I never remember the answers or even that I have asked before. My brain has decided that some things aren't worth saving in a file. Apparently, the fact that my mom had this man's information was one of those things.

However, my brain decided it was worth saving this time. A few days later, I asked my mom for his contact information.

She had his address but wasn't sure if it was still valid. So she called the company where he had worked back in 2005 and found he still worked there.

"I had to explain to the woman in human resources why I wanted this random employee's address," my mom told me. "The woman started crying and gave it to me."

I wonder how often someone in HR receives that sort of request!

The man's name was John. It didn't take me long to write him a letter. The words came flooding out. I thanked him and gave him an update on my life's journey following my assault. I didn't request a response. I just wanted to thank him.

I wasn't even sure he would remember me.

A week later, I got a call from an unknown number. It was John.

"Hi, Carrie. It's John. I got your letter. Of course I remember you," he said. "I think about you all the time. I'm so glad to know you're OK."

Hearing his voice made me remember when my dad brought me to visit John a week after my assault. Since I had left John shirtless at the scene, my dad brought him a shirt. John obviously didn't need it at the time, but the gesture was kind.

John gave me a big hug. I remember he cried.

John and my dad exchanged a handshake with long eye contact. It was a thank-you from one father to another. My dad will probably never admit it, but he is forever grateful that another dad helped out his daughter that night. John told my dad that he had a daughter my age, so this experience hit close to home.

John and I had an instant connection over the phone. We chatted like old friends catching up on life. He asked what I was up to and where I lived.

Then he dropped the C bomb.

John said that two weeks earlier, he had been diagnosed with esophageal and stomach cancer. His prognosis was poor. He was given only a few months left to live. His dad and brother had had the same cancer and didn't live more than three months after receiving the diagnosis. He was scheduled to start chemo and radiation the following week, but he seemed unsure about it.

I got off the phone and sat in silence. Then I started crying and yelling at God.

"Why did you bring him back into my life, only to see him suffer and eventually die? I can't handle seeing him die!"

But then something sparked inside me. I felt the strong desire to save his life like he had saved mine. I was going to be his angel through this.

I asked John if I could visit him. He said he'd love to see me, but he didn't have a lot of free time, with daily doctor appointments, chemo, and radiation.

So the first time I saw John in twelve years was at one of his chemo appointments. I sat in the lobby of the outpatient cancer center and waited for him to come in. I went to the bathroom twice in fifteen minutes. (I'm a nervous pee-er.)

I was so nervous that I wouldn't recognize him, that we wouldn't have anything to talk about. Mostly, I was nervous that I wouldn't be able to handle it emotionally. I feared I would have to run out.

I kept looking out the window, hoping I would recognize him. After a while, I sent him a text message.

"I'm already in back getting my medication started," he texted in reply. "Come on back."

The receptionist helped direct me back there. Then I pulled back a curtain and saw his face. He looked exactly the same as how I remembered him, except for a few more wrinkles and gray hair.

The connection was palpable in the air. He asked if he could give me a hug. I wanted nothing more at that moment than to physically connect with my guardian angel. He was back in my life. And I was going to save him.

I visited John a few more times, and we chatted on the phone regularly. He liked jokes, and I had to learn when he was joking and when he wasn't. He texted me jokes all the time. I was amazed at his outlook and perspective on life as he was fighting to stay alive.

John went into remission six months later, in the fall. When he told me this news, I sighed with relief. I had done my job of saving him. God had answered my prayers.

The following summer, John started losing weight and having immense pain. He got some narcotics from a friend to help with the pain. He refused to go to the doctor. I encouraged him to go and at least get proper medication to help him feel better.

"The pain comes and goes," he said. "And for the most part, it's not bad. I just have some bad days."

But the bad days became more frequent. He started struggling to eat and drink due to the pain in his stomach. John knew the cancer was back—he just didn't want to hear the prognosis. He pushed out going to the doctor as long as he could.

We both knew he was going to die, but we didn't know how long he had.

In early September, I was returning home from vacation when I got a text from John. My plane had just landed in Minneapolis, and I had just turned on my phone.

"I'm not sure when you're back from your trip," John wrote, "but I want you to know that I'm in the hospital and they're telling me I have 2-4 weeks left to live."

I felt my heart physically sink into my gut. I started crying on the airplane.

I sensed my desperation. He *couldn't* leave me. I *needed* him. I needed my guardian angel.

I called him on my way home at ten o'clock at night and asked if it was too late to come visit. He said no, but then my mom talked me into going the next day. I had spent over twenty-four hours traveling, and I was kind of hysterical.

I slept a little that night, only because I was so exhausted from traveling. I woke up with a hollow pit in my stomach.

This may be the last time I see John.

I walked into his hospital room. Immediately, I felt a little uplifted because he looked pretty good. He was in good spirits and joking around as usual, even though they had put a feeding tube in his stomach and he had lost a lot of weight.

He was confused by the prognosis. He didn't understand why the oncologist wouldn't start chemo again or why they wouldn't operate.

John gave the nurse permission to show me his CT scan results, which indicated he had cancer everywhere. I explained to John that was the reason they wouldn't operate — it wouldn't make a difference. Plus, he was too weak. I also explained that chemo wouldn't be enough either. The cancer had spread too far.

He seemed to understand but said, "I feel good. I just don't believe that I have a month left to live."

He joked that if he made it past the four-week prognosis, he would have a party.

John went home from the hospital a few days later. He was technically started on hospice but was still hooking up his feeding tube to get nutrition. He also remained full code, which, in John's words, meant: "If I'm about to die, I want them to do everything they can to save me. It's probably a long shot, but why not give it one last chance?"

That was his mindset with the cancer: don't stop fighting. This was why he was angry with his doctor for "signing off" on him.

I visited him frequently and called every few days to check in. Once he made it four weeks, I asked him when the party was starting.

He struggled a little with the thought of dying, only because he hadn't finished everything he wanted to do in life. He talked about going on a cruise; he'd never been on one. I was serious when I said, "I'll take you on a cruise."

John didn't have the best relationship with his kids. His son had visited him in the hospital, but I never saw his daughter. I was relieved, then, when his daughter moved in with him after he got home from the hospital. She cooked for him even though he couldn't eat much, measured out his liquid narcotic pain medication, and set a timer for how often he could take it.

I was having a hard time imagining John dying. He was getting thinner but remained in good spirits. He was adamant that he wanted to clean up the leaves in his yard. I laughed when he told me over the phone that his daughter wouldn't let him do it. I heard her yelling in the background, "No, because you need rest! You shouldn't be out raking leaves!"

John was determined to continue living his life. He even went as far as trying to buy medication from someone in Mexico who could apparently heal cancer.

John loved good food. That's why his version of cancer was so unfortunate—it impacted his ability to swallow, and any amount of food in his stomach caused pain.

He talked about food a lot and had enjoyed cooking. I once mentioned that I was making soup in a slow cooker, and he asked numerous questions about the ingredients and spices. He was living vicariously through me in those moments.

The last time I saw John was on a Sunday afternoon. I visited at his house like usual, but he didn't get out of bed. He kept himself hooked up to the feeding tube, saying he was trying to get up to the max the doctor had recommended.

He was beyond the definition of skinny. He pulled up his shirt, and I could see every bone in his body. He laughed and joked about his physique.

I was craving comfort food. I didn't realize it, but it was my body's reaction to the reality of John's situation. My body knew the situation was bad, but my mind hadn't fully accepted it yet.

John recommended I get the new cornmeal pizza crust at Pizza Hut. I placed an order for a large pizza, since that was the only size available for the special crust. I planned to pick it up on my way home.

Before heading out, I hugged John as usual. I remember feeling like I was going to break him.

I called my mom after leaving his house. "John's declining," I told her. "He's not getting out of bed much, and he's getting weak."

Once I picked up the pizza, I ate two-thirds of it before I even got home. That's when my body and mind finally connected. I knew the end was near. My guess was that he had only a few weeks left.

I called John that Thursday to check in. After sharing more jokes and laughing about his handsome physique, he said, "Are we still on for the twenty-ninth?"

That was the following Tuesday, when I would be presenting to the Emergency Nurses Association (ENA) about my sexual assault. I had previously invited him to hear me speak, though I knew he might be too weak to come.

I told him that as we got closer to Tuesday, we could talk about how he was feeling.

"I'll see you this weekend," I said.

I was planning to visit John on Saturday but ended up hanging out with a friend. On Sunday, I took a nap in the afternoon because I was coming down with a cold.

After I woke, I called John's number so I could tell him I was heading up to visit him. His daughter answered instead.

John had died Saturday night.

His daughter explained what had happened. While John was resting, she went out to the shed (John's man cave) to have a few minutes alone. She didn't plan to fall asleep, but she did.

Back in the house, John had a breathing attack. He had them frequently near the end. He would get anxious and breathless. It's a natural part of dying. With this attack, John called 911. He was somewhat coherent as the paramedics brought him into the ambulance and started CPR.

Twenty minutes or so later, his daughter woke up to paramedics banging on the door. They told her what had happened—and that John didn't make it.

"I'm so sorry, Carrie," she said. "Know that he loved you so much."

After hanging up, I crumpled to the floor and started crying. "Why did you take him from me?" I yelled at God. "Why couldn't I save him? How am I supposed to live without him?"

I started to have a panic attack. But after a few minutes, I suddenly felt a presence in my house. I stopped crying. It felt like I was getting an imaginary hug. John was there, and he was comforting me.

I knew I was going to be OK.

I called his daughter two days later. I needed to learn more about what had happened. I couldn't understand why he had died so suddenly. I knew he was declining, but I didn't think it would happen that fast.

His daughter said he had seemed fine that Saturday. She explained that she handed him a notebook, telling him to write her a letter. Since the day he'd gotten sick, she'd been asking him to write this letter so she could get it tattooed on her body.

Instead of a letter, he wrote a funny joke: "Have a mint day." It was also the last text he sent me. He came up with these random phrases and thought they were hilarious.

His daughter told me that he then ordered them food from a nice restaurant. They ate spaghetti and garlic bread plus cheesecake for dessert.

"I hadn't seen him eat that much in a long time," she said.

Hearing all this, it was suddenly so clear to me. He knew it was time for him to die, and he chose how and when it would happen.

"John planned to die that night," I explained. "He had a wonderful day with his daughter, ordered his last meal, then waited until you were out of the house so you wouldn't have to see him go."

Even though it was clear that John had deliberately waited for her to leave, she still felt guilty about it—just as I felt guilty for not visiting him on Saturday.

"Dad told me that when you left last Sunday, you gave him a big hug, like, tighter than usual," she told me. "He asked me, 'Does she know something I don't know?'"

I felt uplifted and at peace. In John's mind, that *was* my goodbye.

Over the next few weeks, John visited me several times. Sometimes I would even ask him to come. Every time he came, I felt calm and peaceful.

The following weekend, John's family held a celebration of life at a local bar where John used to hang out. It was such an honor to attend. I was nervous, though, because I was going alone, and I would recognize only his son and daughter. My mom was out of town; otherwise she would have joined me.

I got there thirty minutes after it started. John's son gave me a big hug when he saw me, and then he introduced me to John's siblings. His sister started crying when she saw me.

"John talked about you all the time," she said. "You meant so much to him. He was always in good spirits after talking with you or after you had visited."

She then introduced me to some other family members. Everyone knew who I was. If they didn't know me by name, they knew me by my story: "Remember? This is the girl John helped many years ago."

I spent a long time talking with John's son. He was pretty drunk and uninhibited.

The son played baseball, and he told me how John had missed almost every game. "The games he did come to, he was drunk," the son said. And John didn't seem to care when his son made it on a minor league team.

John had told me about his struggle with alcohol and drugs. He said he'd driven drunk a lot and gone to work drunk. A lot of his drinking coincided with his divorce. His wife had turned to drugs and was no longer the person he had married. Going to treatment helped him get out of his depression, which was fueling the need to drink to feel better.

I had never heard this version of the story, though, where John's drinking impacted his ability to be a good father. But it made sense.

The son said he didn't particularly *like* John, but it was obvious that he missed him. He felt guilty about not being there for John's death. That Saturday, the son had wanted to stay and take care of John, but John insisted he go bowling with his friends. The son was confused about why.

I shared my perspective about the sequence of events and how John had planned to die that night, with no one around.

Hearing this, John's son didn't say much. He just looked surprised.

Pain swept into my heart as I looked at the son — in that moment, I saw the hurting boy inside. From the life journey he shared with me that night, I could tell that all he'd ever wanted was his dad to love him and tell him he was proud.

"I'm not saying that I'm jealous or anything," the son told me, "but he definitely loved you and would have done anything for you."

It dawned on me that I had seen a very different side of John that no one else had gotten to see. I saw the caring, selfless, kindhearted person he was. But his family and kids saw an angry, unable-to-cope alcoholic who cared only about himself. John wasn't perfect, and he wasn't a good dad. He burned a lot of bridges with his family.

I got a lot of surprised but hopeful looks when I shared my perspective about John to his family that night.

I was able to give them a different memory of their dad, brother, brother-in-law, and uncle.

In return, it was healing for me to hear what John had said about me and how much influence I'd made in his life.

"He lit up every time he talked about you," his daughter told me. "He loved the pieces out of you."

His son said that when John's cancer was first diagnosed, John didn't have the drive to continue living. He just accepted the fact that he would die soon.

"But after he got off the phone with you that day two weeks later, he changed," the son declared. "He told me, 'I want to get to know her.' He had a reason to live. And that's why he was so insistent on doing chemo and radiation and beating this."

I stood there in shock as I listened to this testimony of how I had impacted John's life. A major reason John lived as long as he did was because of *me*. I had given him hope and a reason to live. And through the process, he was able to rekindle a semblance of a relationship with his kids.

I finally felt at peace. I wasn't able to save his life, but I did make a difference in it.

L ooking at my story and at John's, the sequence of events is far from coincidental.

I was abducted, raped, and stabbed, then my life was saved by a random stranger.

I changed careers and became a nurse.

I worked as a sexual assault nurse examiner, providing the same care I had received that night.

I was given the chance to live out of state and become comfortable with unknown places.

I began speaking publicly about my experience—after ten years of not being able to talk about it.

I went on mission trips to provide care for the underserved population in Haiti.

I got a doctorate in nursing so I could have the skill set to impact the lives of many patients.

At a speaking event, my brain finally retained the information about my mom having John's contact information.

I had the strength to reach out to John.

He had been diagnosed with cancer two weeks prior to receiving my letter.

I was able to reconnect with him and develop a relationship with this father figure and guardian angel in my life.

I helped him find the hope and strength to treat his cancer and go into remission, adding months to his life.

I helped bring John and his kids closer together.

And I was able to metaphorically save his life, like he had saved mine.

God works in mysterious ways. I know that God didn't intend for me to get abducted, raped, and stabbed. But God has used that experience for good in so many ways.

I was scheduled to speak at the ENA conference three days after John's death. I asked his son and daughter if they wanted to attend, because I shared a lot about John during this particular speech.

His son came and sat in the back of the room. I planned to ask him to stand in recognition as I spoke about John.

The thing is, my vision goes completely blurry when I get to the part in my presentation where I share my story. Then it instantly clears once I finish my story and continue with the rest of the presentation. So when I asked John's son to stand up, my vision was still blurry, but it started clearing as I looked up from the page I was reading.

In that moment, I saw John standing in the back of the room, smiling at me. He had come to hear me speak and had given me the strength to get through it.

I think about John often and I miss him. But I know that God has a lot of jobs for him in heaven as an angel, including visiting me and his kids when we need comfort and peace.

John's time on earth has ended, but mine hasn't. God has given me the strength to continue sharing my story and to write this book. God still has a lot more planned for me until I can see John again in heaven.

ACKNOWLEDGMENTS

Finishing this book would have been impossible without the support of my family, especially my mom. She has been my rock throughout my healing journey. She never gets impatient when I repeatedly ask the same questions. She debriefs with me every time I present my testimony and has recently started presenting with me. Her version of the story is very different, but we have the same emotions dealing with trauma. We have an unbreakable, special bond, having both been through the trauma of sexual assault. I know that she has continued in her healing journey with me as I've written this book.

I want to thank the sexual assault program coordinator at HCMC, who encouraged me to share my testimony for the first time; the many others who provided me with a venue and safe space to present; and the listeners who heard my testimony and encouraged me to write a book about my story.

I am grateful for my editor, Angie Wiechmann; proofreader, Ruthie Nelson; and publisher, Ann Aubitz, for making my aimless words on a page authentically represent who I am and who I've become.

Lastly, I want to acknowledge my angel, John, and his family. Such a unique connection between two strangers doesn't happen very often. I am fortunate to have had this experience with John and a relationship with his family as a result.

ABOUT THE AUTHOR

D r. Carrie Manke is an advanced practice nurse working in a hospital emergency department. She is passionate about advocating for survivors, helping others recover from trauma and PTSD, and ending domestic and sexual abuse. She frequently speaks on these subjects and is available for presentations, lectures, or readings of the book. To learn more, visit **carriemanke.com**